Science

Making Healthy Decisions
Nutrition

Unit 1

BSCS

KENDALL/HUNT PUBLISHING COMPANY
4050 Westmark Drive   Dubuque, Iowa 52002

ADVISORY COMMITTEE
Lawrence W. Green
Donald C. Iverson
Lloyd J. Kolbe
Nathan Maccoby
Katharine G. Sommers

BSCS PROJECT STAFF
Nancy M. Landes, Project Director and Revision Coordinator, Final Edition
James D. Ellis, Project Director, Field-test Edition
Rodger W. Bybee, Contributing Author
Joseph D. McInerney, Contributing Author
Susan Frelick Wooley, Contributing Author
Teresa T. Hendrickson, Editor, Field-test Edition
C. Yvonne Wise, Editor, Final Edition
Jan Girard, Art Coordinator
Byllee Simon, Senior Executive Assistant

WRITING TEAMS, FIELD-TEST EDITIONS
Katherine A. Corley, Middle School Teacher
Sandra L.H. Davenport, M.D.
Ann Junk, Middle School Teacher
Terry Shaw, Middle School Teacher
David R. Stronck, Health Educator
Gordon Thies, Health Educator
Gordon E. Uno, Science Educator

REVIEWERS, FIELD-TEST EDITIONS
Steven N. Blair
Glen Gilbert
Gilda Gussin
Louise Light
Peter D. Loranger
Richard R.J. Lauzon
Terry Shaw
David A. Sleet

BSCS ADMINISTRATIVE STAFF
Timothy H. Goldsmith, Chair, Board of Directors
Joseph D. McInerney, Director
Lawrence Satkowiak, Chief Financial Officer

FIELD-TEST SCHOOLS
Challenger Middle School, Colorado Springs, Colorado
Aspen Middle School, Aspen, Colorado
Buffalo Ridge Elementary School, Grade 6, Laramie, Wyoming
Calhan Elementary School, Grade 6, Calhan, Colorado
Carver Elementary School, Grade 6, Colorado Springs, Colorado
Kearney Middle School, Commerce City, Colorado
Ortega Middle School, Alamosa, Colorado
Sabin Junior High School, Colorado Springs, Colorado
Sproul Junior High School, Widefield, Colorado
Webster Elementary School, Grade 6, Widefield, Colorado
Widefield Elementary School, Grade 6, Widefield, Colorado
Watson Junior High School, Widefield, Colorado

ARTISTS/PHOTOGRAPHERS
Susan Bartle
Brenda Bundy
Carlye Calvin
Jan Girard
Nancy Smalls
Linn Trochim

ISBN 0-7872-1206-7

This work was supported by the Gates Foundation, the Helen K. and Arthur E. Johnson Foundation, the Piton Foundation, and the Adolph Coors Foundation. However, the opinions expressed herein do not necessarily reflect the position or policies of the funding agencies, and no official endorsement should be inferred.

10 9 8 7 6 5 4 3 2 1

TABLE OF CONTENTS

UNIT 1: NUTRITION

FOREWORD

Whether you are aware of it or not, you make decisions about your health all day, every day. You are making decisions about your health when you decide what to eat for breakfast or whether to eat breakfast at all, whether to brush and floss your teeth, whether to wear a safety belt if you ride to school in a car, how to communicate with your classmates and teachers once you arrive at school, what to eat for lunch, whether to participate in sports or exercise after school, which television programs you watch, and when you go to sleep. Believe it or not, just about everything you do has some impact on your health and YOU are in charge of most of those decisions. Are the decisions you make healthy ones? How do you know? Do you care?

Sometimes, it's tough to make healthy decisions. All of us have lots of excuses: It's not what my friends are doing. I'm not sick, so why worry about what I eat? I'm careful, so I'm not going to get hurt. I really don't have time to exercise. No one else in the car has on a safety belt. In the lessons you are about to experience, we hope to convince you that it makes sense to pay attention to your health while you're healthy. Although some of the actions you take might not have an effect until years later, many decisions will make a difference right now in how you feel, how you relate to your friends and family, whether or not you become injured, whether you contract a life-threatening illness, or whether you put someone else's life and health at risk.

We sincerely hope you enjoy the activities in this unit of *Making Healthy Decisions* and that they make a difference in how you care for yourself and those around you. Remember, the healthy decisions are up to you.

Nancy M. Landes
Revision Director

James D. Ellis
Project Director
Field-test Edition

INTRODUCTION TO NUTRITION

Junk food...fast food...empty-calorie food...high-fiber food...iron-fortified food. Which foods are really good for you? Are all the good-tasting foods always bad for your health? Does it really matter all that much what you eat?

The reality is that it *does* matter what you eat, at least if you want to be in good shape and stay healthy. Eating a nutritious diet doesn't mean that you have to go without foods that you really like. Each food you eat won't make you healthy or unhealthy, but over time, too much of some kinds of foods and too little of others can put your health at risk. What's important is eating a *balance* of foods that give you enough energy to be active and enough nutrients so your body can grow, repair injuries, and keep working the way it should.

In this unit, you will learn a lot about the foods you eat—which ones are high in fat, which ones are low in fat and still taste good, which foods you can eat as much of and as often as you like. You will learn which foods at your favorite fast-food restaurant are healthier choices than others and will learn to categorize foods as "Anytime," "Sometimes," and "Seldom" according to how often you should eat them. You will be able to help your family and friends read food labels so you can find good-tasting, healthy choices at the grocery store. You will even have a chance to influence what the school cafeteria serves for lunch!

What and how much you eat and how often you exercise determine to a great extent how you feel each and every day. If you often skip meals, grab a quick candy bar for lunch and a quick burger for dinner, fill up on lots of snacks, and dance up and down on the diet yo-yo, then this unit is for you! By paying attention to what you eat, you can improve both how you look and how you feel. The choice is yours! Here's to happy, healthy eating...

MAKING CHOICES

Before your school day begins, you have made many choices. You have decided when to get up, what to wear, how to style your hair, whether to eat breakfast, what to eat for breakfast, how to get to school, or how to get to a friend's house before school. Throughout the day, you continue to make choices. You probably make many choices without thinking much about them.

Some of the choices you make each day are about the food you eat. Have you ever thought about what influences your choice of food? Do you eat mainly what you are used to eating? what your friends eat? what your family eats? what is placed in front of you? what you can grab quickly? what tastes the best? what is healthiest for you? Many things impact the food choices you make. Hopefully, this and the lessons that follow will influence you to think more carefully about what you eat and why.

ACTIVITY: HEALTHY OR UNHEALTHY FOR YOU?

Has anyone ever suggested that you eat a food because it was healthy for you? Has anyone ever said that you shouldn't eat something because it would not be "good for you"? What do you already know about which foods are healthy or unhealthy for you? In this lesson, you and your classmates will find out what you think about the foods you eat. Are they healthy or unhealthy for you and why?

Healthy or Unhealthy?

Procedure

1. Make a chart by dividing a sheet of 11" x 17" construction paper into three sections. As headings for the sections, write "Healthy Foods" at the top of the left-hand section, "Somewhat Healthy Foods" at the top of the middle section, and "Unhealthy Foods" at the top of the right-hand section.

   To make your chart, draw two vertical lines on the paper, one line about 6 inches from each edge of the paper as shown below.

HEALTHY FOODS	SOMEWHAT HEALTHY FOODS	UNHEALTHY FOODS

2. In magazines and newspapers, find pictures of foods you eat and cut them out.

   Throughout this unit, the term "food" includes both solid foods and beverages (drinks). Because most beverages (except water) contain calories and often provide vitamins, minerals, and other nutrients, they are considered food for your body.

3.   Glue each picture onto your chart under the heading where you think each food belongs. *Within each section, you can arrange your pictures to form a collage, an artistic collection of images that might overlap or relate to one another in some way.*

4.   Review your completed chart and be prepared to explain your placement of the pictures of the foods. *What made you decide that some foods were more or less healthy than others? Do some foods have certain things that others do not? Are some foods missing certain ingredients that make them more or less healthy for you?*

5.   Compare your chart with your classmates charts and discuss any differences in the placement of similar foods. *Did everyone put the same foods under the same headings? Which foods were the easiest or the most difficult to place? Why were there differences of opinion?*

Stop and Discuss

1.   What do "healthy" foods have that other foods do not have? Write those things on a chart titled "Healthy Foods Have."

2.   What do "somewhat healthy" or "unhealthy" foods contain that healthy foods do not? Write those ideas on a chart titled "Less Healthy Foods Have."

3.   How often do you choose foods based on how healthy you think those foods are for you? What else influences your choices of foods to eat?

WRAP UP

During the next week, make a list of the foods served in the school cafeteria each day. Bring the list to class and rate the foods as "healthy," "somewhat healthy," or "unhealthy." Discuss why you classified the foods as you did and present your ratings to the cafeteria manager or principal. Present healthier alternatives that the school cafeteria could offer. Suggest only those foods that you think students would like to eat.

INVOLVING FAMILY MEMBERS

Write a letter to your family members inviting them to become involved in the study of nutrition. Share the chart you made in class and invite them to think about the choices they make in the foods they eat at home and at work. What influences their choices: taste, nutrition, customs, cost, availability, ease of preparation? What do they think makes some foods healthier or less healthy than others? Nutrition is a family affair, and you can help one another make healthy decisions about the foods you eat.

LESSON 2

HOW SWEET IT IS

When you made your charts in Lesson 1, what made you decide that some foods were less healthy than others? Was something missing in the less healthy foods? Or, could it be that those foods had something extra that the healthy foods did not? Could it be....could it be.... too much SUGAR??!!??

ACTIVITY: BECOMING A SUGAR SLEUTH

Procedure

1. Read the list of ingredients from the following food packages.
2. Decide which food has the most sugar. *Be prepared to give reasons for your answer.*
3. On a piece of scrap paper, write the name of the food that you think has the most sugar, along with two reasons explaining why you chose that food.

NUTRITION FACTS

<u>Ingredients:</u> Corn, sugar, corn syrup, molasses, salt, annatto color.

Food #1

NUTRITION FACTS

<u>Ingredients:</u> Whole oat flour (with oat bran), whole wheat flour, sugar, maltodextrin, malted barley extract, molasses, brown sugar, baking soda, salt.

Food #2

NUTRITION FACTS

<u>Ingredients:</u> Sugar, wheat, corn syrup, honey, hydrogenated soybean oil, caramel color, salt.

Food #3

READING: THE MANY DISGUISES OF THAT SUGARY CHARACTER

When you looked at the lists of ingredients, how many times did you see the word "sugar"? Was that the only clue you used to decide which food actually had the most sugar? If you used other clues, then you are indeed a sugar sleuth.

Clue Number 1: Sugar has many disguises, aliases, assumed names, and a.k.a.'s.* Look at the lists of ingredients again. Which words do you think might be some of sugar's other names? Which ingredients do you think of as sweet or that could be used as a "sweetener"?

(*The letters *a.k.a.* stand for "also known as" and is a phrase used in police and detective work to describe another name for a person or thing.)

If you suggested corn syrup, brown sugar, or corn sweetener, you are right! Those are just some of sugar's other names. A more complete list includes the following:

brown sugar	honey
corn sweetener	malt
corn syrup	maltose
dextrose	maple syrup
fructose	molasses
glucose	sucrose

Any of these names indicates that sugar is in the food. Because you see an assumed name for sugar in a list of ingredients, does that mean that you should not eat that food? Not necessarily. We'll tell you more about that later.

Clue Number 2: The order in which you find sugar (or another name for sugar) in the list of ingredients does matter. So that food labels can help people make decisions about the foods they eat, the United States Food and Drug Administration (USFDA) provides food companies rules to follow. The USFDA requires that all lists of ingredients on food labels show the ingredients in order by weight. This means that the first ingredient is what there is the most of in that food. The second ingredient on the list is the second most common item in the food. The list continues until the label shows all the ingredients in the food. The ingredient listed last is the one found in the smallest amount (by weight) in that food.

This information will make more sense to you after you complete the next activity, "Making Sense of Nutrition Facts."

ACTIVITY: MAKING SENSE OF NUTRITION FACTS

Procedure

1.   On a piece of paper, draw the following data table:

Number of Food	Name(s) for Sugar Found in the List of Ingredients	Rank Order in the List of Ingredients (first, second, third...)

2.   Complete the data table for each of the foods in "Becoming a Sugar Sleuth."
       List each name for sugar and its position in the list of ingredients. For example, was this type of sugar listed first, third, seventh, tenth, or in some other position in the list of ingredients?
3.   Using the information from the data table, decide which food has the most sugar. Circle the sample number of the food you selected as having the most sugar.
4.   Below the data table, write the reasons why you selected that food as having the most sugar.
       Use information from the data table to support your conclusion.
5.   Compare your answer from this activity with your choice from "Becoming a Sugar Sleuth."
       Did you select the same food as having the most sugar? Which answer is based on good information or "data"?

ACTIVITY: WHICH ONE WOULD YOU CHOOSE?

Procedure

1.   Number your paper from 1 through 7. Beside each number, write the type of food from the following data table that corresponds with each number.
       For example, you would write "applesauce" beside number 1 on your paper.
2.   Read the list of ingredients from Product A and from Product B for each type of food listed.
3.   Decide which food, Product A or Product B, has <u>less sugar</u>, and write "A" or "B" on your paper to indicate which product you selected.
       Pay attention to the number of times you see the word "sugar" or another name for sugar in each list and notice the position of each of those words in the list.
4.   Next to your selection of "A" or "B," write the reason or reasons why you selected Product A or Product B for each type of food.

Data Table Comparing Food Products

Type of Food	List of Ingredients	
	Product A	**Product B**
1. Applesauce	apples, water, and salt	apples, high fructose corn syrup, corn syrup, sugar, water, lemon juice and spice, erythorbic acid added to protect color
2. Peanut Butter	peanuts, contains 2% or less of salt	selected U.S. fresh roasted peanuts, sugar, hydrogenated vegetable oil (contains rapeseed; cottonseed; and soybean oils), peanut oil, salt, molasses, and monoglycerides
3. Canned Beans	beans, water, sugar, corn syrup, bacon (cured with water, salt, sodium phosphate, hydrolyzed soy protein, sodium erythorbate, artificial maple flavor, sodium nitrite), brown sugar, salt, modified food starch, cornstarch, dextrose, spice, caramel color, onion powder, whey, hickory smoked torula yeast, white pepper, mustard flour, garlic powder, liquid smoke, natural smoke flavoring	prepared black beans, water, and salt
4. Salad Dressing	soybean oil, water, sugar, vinegar, salt, mustard flour, paprika, xanthan gum, propylene glycol alginate, natural flavor, calcium disodium EDTA as a preservative, apocarotenol (color)	high fructose corn syrup, soybean oil, vinegar, tomato paste, water, salt, paprika, spices, propylene glycolalginate, natural flavors, color added, calcium disodium EDTA to maintain quality

5. Cereal	whole oat flour (includes the oat bran), sugar, defatted wheat germ, wheat starch, honey, brown sugar syrup, salt, ground almonds, trisodium phosphate, vitamin E (mixed tocopherols) added to preserve freshness, vitamins and minerals	whole oat flour (includes the oat bran), modified food starch, wheat starch, sugar, salt, oat fiber, trisodium phosphate, calcium carbonate, vitamin E (mixed tocopherols) added to preserve freshness, vitamins and minerals
6. Spaghetti Sauce	crushed tomatoes, tomato puree (water, tomato paste), corn syrup, parmesan cheese, soybean oil, onions, salt, garlic powder, romano cheese, parsley, spices	diced tomatoes, tomato puree (water, tomato paste), onions, garlic, pure olive oil, salt, basil, black pepper
7. Crackers	whole wheat, vegetable oil (partially hydrogenated soybean oil), salt	enriched wheat flour, bleached wheat flour, vegetable shortening (partially hydrogenated soybean oil), whole wheat, rice, rolled oats, brown sugar, degermed yellow corn meal, sugar, oat bran, barley flakes, salt, high fructose corn syrup, leavening, modified corn starch, whey, onion powder, malted barley syrup, soy lecithin, malted barley flour

READING: WHAT'S WRONG WITH SUGAR?

What difference does it make whether you choose foods that have a lot of sugar or those that don't have as much? Is sugar really all that unhealthy? There are three basic problems with eating foods high in sugar.

Problem #1: Empty calories. Alone sugar (in all its forms) is not unhealthy. The real issue is that sugar contains nothing except energy, or calories. Sugar does not have any vitamins, minerals, or other nutrients, so nutritionists (people who know a lot about nutrition and what is good for us to eat) sometimes refer to foods with a lot of sugar as "empty-calorie" foods. "Empty-calorie" foods have calories but few nutrients—the good things your body needs to stay healthy.

A part of this problem is that most of the sugar you eat is added to foods before you buy them. (Remember all the evidence of sugar you found in the lists of ingredients from the previous activities?) According to research reports, sugar is a leading ingredient added to foods in the United States. Because of this, most people have no idea how much sugar they actually eat. Many people think that if they are not adding sugar to their food, they are not eating very much sugar. Would you believe that most Americans eat about 130 pounds of sugar each year? That's a lot of sugar and a lot of empty calories!

Problem #2: The sugar and fat connection. You usually don't eat sugar by itself. Often, foods that are high in sugar, such as cake, cookies, candy bars, and ice cream, also are high in fat. (You will find out more about foods high in fat the next lesson.) These foods can fill you up (and OUT!) without giving you the vitamins, minerals, and other nutrients you need to stay healthy and fit.

Problem #3: Sugar and your teeth. Eating sugary foods, especially candies that are gooey and stick to your teeth, can be harmful to your teeth and gums. When you have a lot of sugar in your mouth and around your teeth, the bacteria in your mouth feed on the sugar and produce acids that can cause cavities (dental caries) and gum disease. This is the largest—and most expensive—problem with children and adolescents who eat high sugar foods. So, if you want to reduce the amount of drilling by the dentist, read the lists of ingredients, avoid foods with lots of sugar, and brush your teeth at least twice a day.

Stop and Discuss

1. How can reading the lists of ingredients on food packages help you cut down on sugar?
2. What do you need to remember about the lists of ingredients that will help you choose foods lower in sugar?
3. Why might you want to eat less sugar?
4. What foods do you like that would provide tasty alternatives to foods high in sugar?

WRAP UP

Collect the labels from many different cereal packages. Read the lists of ingredients from those cereal labels and, using the information from the labels, rank the cereals from those with the most sugar to those with the least. Which cereals do you usually eat? Where do they rank in terms of sugar content? Would you be willing to try some of the cereals that have less sugar?

INVOLVING FAMILY MEMBERS

Share the information about sugar and ingredients lists with your family members. Ask them to compare the lists of ingredients on packages of cereals, crackers, or other types of food and to discuss which have more or less sugar. Accompany your parents or guardians to the grocery store and help select foods that are low in sugar. Try those foods and decide which ones family members would be willing to substitute for those high in sugar. (Don't forget that some of the lowest sugar foods are ones, such as fresh fruits and vegetables, that don't have any lists of ingredients!)

LOSING THE FAT

ACTIVITY: MAKING HEALTHY CHOICES

Procedure

1. One at a time, compare the following pairs of foods in Lists A and B.
2. For each pair, decide which food you would rather eat—the one in List A or the one in List B.
3. On a piece of scrap paper, write the name of that food.
    To organize your answers, you might write the letters A through G on the left side of your paper.
4. Next, decide which food in each pair would be healthier for you.
5. Next to the food you chose in Step 2, write the name of the food choice you think is healthier.
    The names of the foods you write might be the same as in Step 2 or they might be different.
6. Compare your answers.

Food Choices

	List A	List B
A.	potato chips	plain baked potato
B.	ice cream	low-fat yogurt
C.	a hamburger	baked chicken
D.	pizza with cheese and sausage	pizza with cheese only
E.	butter (on bread in a sandwich)	mustard (on bread in a sandwich)
F.	a cheeseburger	a tuna fish sandwich
G.	a candy bar	fresh fruit

1. Which list contains the healthier foods?
2. Which would you rather eat, the foods in List A or the foods in List B? Why did you choose those foods?
3. Why are the foods in one list not as healthy as the foods in the other list? Do they have anything in common?

READING: RISKS FROM A HIGH-FAT DIET

The main reason that the foods in List A are not as healthy is because they all have a lot of fat. (Some, such as ice cream and candy bars, also have a lot of sugar.) Eating too many high-fat foods can lead to some health problems. One of the major risks from a high-fat diet is eating too many calories, gaining too much body fat and becoming overweight. The following illustration will show you why that can be a problem.

If you exercise regularly, you do not have to worry as much about gaining weight or extra body fat from the calories you eat. However, if you eat a lot of high-fat foods, it is more difficult to maintain your weight even with regular exercise.

Another problem with eating too many foods that are high in fats is the development of a disease called atherosclerosis. The pictures below show what atherosclerosis is.

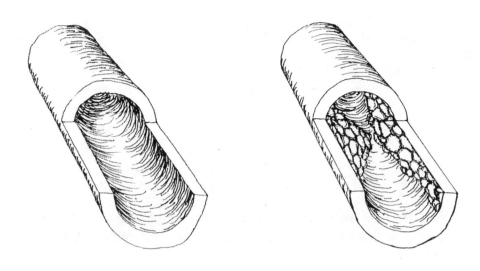

The blood carries fatty particles called "cholesterol." Sometimes, extra cholesterol is deposited or put down in the blood vessels, usually in your arteries. These blood vessels then become very narrow because they have a lining of cholesterol or plaque. The heart has difficulty pumping blood through those narrow tubes.

Imagine the empty cardboard tube from a roll of paper towels. If you blew through the empty tube, air would pass through easily. If you gradually lined the tube with pieces of paper, what would happen? The first few sheets of paper would hardly make a difference. But, after 20 or 50 pieces of paper, the opening in the tube would become narrow. Then, you couldn't blow as much air through the tube.

The same thing happens when blood vessels become clogged. Eventually, clogged arteries may cause people to have high blood pressure because the blood must squeeze through a very narrow opening. If the clogged blood vessel is one that leads to the heart, a person might have a heart attack or need bypass surgery to prevent a heart attack.

This doesn't mean that everyone who eats high-fat foods will have clogged arteries. It also doesn't mean that you can't ever eat fatty foods. It just means that you need to pay attention to how often you eat foods that are high in fats. The American Heart Association recommends that no more than one-third of all the calories you eat come from fats. So, you don't have to give up ice cream or potato chips forever. You just need to balance the kinds of foods you eat and only eat high-fat foods once in a while, not at every meal.

ACTIVITY: TESTING FOR FATS

How can you tell when foods have a lot of fat? There is a simple test called the "fat rub" that will help you find out.

Procedure

1. On a piece of brown paper bag or butcher paper, make a chart that looks like the following:

Fat Rub Chart

Sample: water	Sample: oil
Raw potato	French fried potato
Baked potato	Potato chip

2. Dip your finger in a cup of water and make a mark next to the word "water."
   Because water contains no fat, this mark will be your sample for a food that has no fat.
3. Dip your finger in a cup of cooking oil and make a mark next to the word "oil."
   Because cooking oil is 100 percent fat, this mark will be your sample for foods that have a lot of fat.
4. Rub a piece of each type of potato in the appropriate section of the chart.
5. Circle the name of each food that has fat.
6. On another piece of brown paper bag or butcher paper, make a new chart and test other foods by rubbing a piece of the food on a section of the bag.
   Be sure to label each mark with the name of the food you rubbed in that space.
7. Circle the name of each food that shows evidence of fat.

Stop and Discuss

1. Compare your results. Which foods left oily marks on the brown paper? Which foods did not?
2. How might you describe foods that have a lot of fats? Do those foods have anything in common?
3. How might you describe foods that do not have fats? Do those foods have anything in common?

READING: LOW-FAT VERSUS HIGH-FAT FOODS

You can't do a "fat rub" on every food you eat, so how can you choose low-fat foods? The following lists might help you choose foods that are lower in fats.

High-fat Foods	Low-fat Foods
Meats	**Meats**
fried chicken	chicken or turkey, baked or broiled without skin
chicken or turkey with skin	canned tuna, packed in water
bacon	fish, broiled or baked
sausage	vegetarian sausage made from soy beans
spare ribs	ground turkey
ham	
regular ground beef or hamburger	
canned tuna, packed in oil	
hot dogs	
beef or pork luncheon or deli meats	
Dairy	**Dairy**
most hard cheeses	reduced fat cheeses
butter	low-fat yogurt
sour cream	sherbet
cream cheese	low-fat milk shakes
whipped cream	cottage cheese (1%)
whole milk	skim or 1% milk
ice cream	Sealtest Free ice cream
Other foods	**Other foods**
eggs	
mayonnaise	light, fat-free mayonnaise
croissants	bread
donuts	potatoes, boiled or baked
pastries	cereal, except granola
cake	rice
pie	peas, beans, or lentils
cookies	fruits
peanuts and peanut butter	most vegetables
coconut	graham crackers
palm oil	pretzels
chocolate	plain popcorn, air popped
potato and corn chips	

1.   What are some characteristics of high-fat foods? (Think about the way they are prepared or what the foods in the high-fat list have in common.)
2.   Which words on a food label might tell you that a food is high in fat? low in fat?

WRAP UP

Not all foods that leave oily marks on brown paper have the same amount of fat. And, not all foods that leave oily marks on brown paper have the same kind of fat. Find out about the differences between saturated fats, polyunsaturated fats, and monounsaturated fats. Ask your media specialist to help you find some good reference books, or invite a nutritionist or another health professional to your class to talk about the differences between the kinds of fat and which foods contain the different kinds of fats.

INVOLVING FAMILY MEMBERS

As a family, make a list of the foods you eat at each evening meal and for snacks after school or before bed. Discuss which foods are low in fat and which might be high in fat. Talk about ways you could add some low-fat foods to your choice of snacks or to the evening meal without giving up all of your favorite foods. Are there ways you could prepare the foods that would reduce the amount of fat?

LESSON 4

SNACK TIME

How would you define a "snack"? The dictionary defines it this way:

> snack/snak/n. Food served or taken informally, usually in small amounts and typically under other circumstances than as a regular meal.

ACTIVITY: MY FAVORITE SNACKS

Procedure

1.   On a piece of paper, list 10 of your favorite snack foods.
     Number your paper from 1 through 10 and write one food beside each number.
2.   Using the following rating scale, rate each of your favorite snacks by writing a number next to the name of the food on your list from Step 1.
     If you are not sure how to rate a snack, make your best guess based on your discussions from the previous lessons about what makes foods healthy, or nutritious.

5	4	3	2	1
Very Nutritious		Somewhat Nutritious		Not Nutritious

3.   Next to the rating number, explain your rating for each food.
     Why did you choose that rating number? Does the food have a lot of sugar? just a little sugar? a lot of fat? little or no fat? a lot of vitamins and minerals? not many calories?
4.   Discuss your list and ratings with a partner.
     Do you agree on the ratings for each snack food on yours and your partner's list? Why or why not?

1. Do you like to eat mainly nutritious or not very nutritious snacks? Why do you make these choices?
2. Do you care if your snack choices are nutritious? Why or why not?
3. What might convince you to eat snacks that are more nutritious?

ACTIVITY: A TASTE TEST

During this activity, you will work with a partner and conduct a taste test of snack foods. One of you will be the "taster," the person who tastes the snack foods. (Because the tasters must concentrate on what they taste and not on what they see, they will be blindfolded during the taste test.) The other partner will be the "feeder," the one who feeds the snack foods to the blindfolded taster. After you and your partner complete one taste test, you will switch roles and the taster becomes the feeder and vice versa. You might find out about some new taste treats during this test.

Taste buds ready? Let's begin.

Procedure

1. Before you begin this activity, wash your hands thoroughly with soap and water.
    This is important because you will be handling food.
2. Select a partner for this activity.
    Your teacher might assign partners for this activity.
3. Decide who will be the "taster" during the first round of this activity and who will be the "feeder." The taster should take a seat, either in a chair or on the floor.
    Remember that you will switch roles after the first round of testing so that each partner will get a turn to be the taster. Because the taster will be blindfolded, he or she must be seated during the activity.
4. Review with your partner a copy of A Taste-Test Rating Sheet.
    You will need two copies of this record page, one for each partner. This rating sheet describes the rating scale for the taste test. Make sure the taster understands the rating scale.
5. Tie a blindfold around the taster's eyes.
    Make sure the taster cannot see below the blindfold.
6. As the feeder, put on the plastic gloves provided or pick up 10 toothpicks. Next, pick up a plate of 10 snack foods or, using toothpicks and serving utensils, select 10 foods from the snack foods available. Also, pick up a copy of Record Page 4.1 A Taste Test Rating Sheet. Carry the snack foods and the Record Page to where your partner is seated.
7. Write your partner's name at the top of the rating sheet.

8.   As the feeder, follow these steps in conducting the taste test:

   a.   Select one snack food to be tasted and write the name of that food in the first column of the record page.
         Be sure to indicate whether the snack food comes with a dressing or dip. For example, you might write "raw apple" or "apple with yogurt dip," depending on which snack you have selected.
   b.   Place a bite-size piece of the selected snack food in the taster's mouth.
   c.   Allow the taster to chew and swallow the food.
   d.   Ask the taster how he or she would rate this snack food.
         If necessary, read the rating scale to the taster.
   e.   In the appropriate space on the record page, record the taster's rating for that food.
   f.   Repeat steps a through d for each of the 10 snack foods.
9.   Switch roles so that the taster becomes the feeder and the feeder becomes the taster. Repeat Steps 4 through 8.
10.   Discuss with your partner your ratings for each snack food.
      For which foods do your ratings agree? For which foods do your ratings disagree? Discuss any differences of opinion.

Stop and Discuss

1.   Compile a class list of the ratings for each snack food and discuss the ratings.
      You might group together all the foods rated "A" by most of your classmates, all those rated "B," and so on.
2.   If you were planning a party and wanted to provide nutritious snacks, which foods from this list would you include? Which would you avoid?
3.   What are some other snacks that you think would be healthy choices?
4.   How might you convince someone in your family to try some of the nutritious snacks you tasted in this activity?
5.   Are many healthy snack foods advertised on television? Why do you think this is so?

WRAP UP

Plan a healthy snacks party or a healthy snacks taste test for a class of younger students. It might be fun to make some of the snacks or special dressings and dips with the younger students as part of the experience. Think about foods that might appeal to younger students and that would be healthy alternatives to some of the snacks they probably eat most of the time.

INVOLVING FAMILY MEMBERS

Take home some of the recipes that your teacher used to make the nutritious snacks for the class "taste test." Try the taste test at home with members of your family or simply make some of the nutritious snacks for everyone to sample. Talk about what makes these snacks more nutritious than other snacks you might choose. Make a family agreement to include at least one nutritious snack food each day. Bring any new ideas and recipes for healthy snacks to class and share them with your classmates and teacher.

HOW DOES YOUR DAILY DIET STACK UP?

ACTIVITY: RATING MY EATING HABITS

Procedure

1.   On a piece of paper, make a data table that looks like this:

<table>
<tr><td colspan="5" align="center">Rating My Eating Habits: Data Table</td></tr>
<tr><td></td><td>Usually,</td><td>Sometimes,</td><td>Not Very Often,</td><td>I Don't Know</td></tr>
<tr><td>A.</td><td>_____</td><td>_____</td><td>_____</td><td>_____</td></tr>
<tr><td>B.</td><td>_____</td><td>_____</td><td>_____</td><td>_____</td></tr>
<tr><td>C.</td><td>_____</td><td>_____</td><td>_____</td><td>_____</td></tr>
<tr><td>D.</td><td>_____</td><td>_____</td><td>_____</td><td>_____</td></tr>
<tr><td>E.</td><td>_____</td><td>_____</td><td>_____</td><td>_____</td></tr>
<tr><td>F.</td><td>_____</td><td>_____</td><td>_____</td><td>_____</td></tr>
</table>

2. Read the following statements, one at a time.
    A. I eat a variety of foods each day.
    B. My weight is about right for my age (not too much and not too little).
    C. I eat a lot of vegetables, fruits, and whole-grain foods.
    D. I avoid foods that are high in fats.
    E. I avoid foods that are high in sugar.
    F. I avoid foods that are high in salt.

3. Following each letter A through F in your data table, place a check mark in the column that shows how often you do what that statement says.
    This is not a test and no one will look at your data table, so be honest. This is a way for you to think about your eating habits. If you really aren't sure if the foods you eat have a lot of sugar, fat, or salt, then check "I Don't Know." You will get more information later.
4. Review your completed data table.
    How many of these statements do you usually follow?

ACTIVITY: EXAMINING THE FOOD GUIDE PYRAMID

Government agencies, such as the U.S. Food and Drug Administration and the U.S. Department of Agriculture, developed a model called the Food Guide Pyramid to help people understand how they might eat a more balanced diet. What does this "pyramid" tell you about how you might select the foods you eat each day? How does it relate to the statements you rated in the first activity of this lesson?

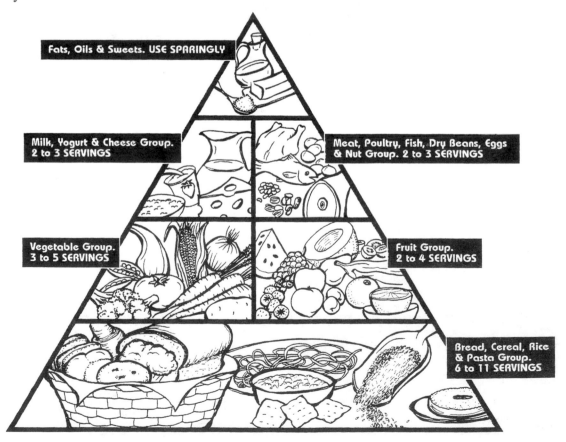

Procedure

1. On a piece of scrap paper, list all the foods you ate yesterday.
    Do the best you can to remember what you had for breakfast, lunch, dinner, and snacks. Remember to include beverages as well as solid foods.
2. Using the categories in the Food Guide Pyramid, classify the foods you listed in Step 1.
    You can do this by writing the pyramid categories and listing the names of the foods you ate within each category or by indicating after each food which pyramid category it fits.
3. How do the foods you ate yesterday "stack up"?
    Did you eat enough servings in the bread, cereal, rice, and pasta category? Did you eat enough fruits and vegetables? Did you eat too many sweets, fats, or oils?

Stop and Discuss

1. What do you think the Food Guide Pyramid tells people about what food choices they should make?
2. Do you think most people follow the Food Pyramid guidelines? Why or why not?
3. Do you think you usually follow the Food Pyramid guidelines? Why or why not?
4. Review the six statements from the first activity "Rating My Eating Habits" and answer these questions: If people ate according to the Food Guide Pyramid, would they be able to answer "usually" to those six statements? Why or why not?

READING: UNDERSTANDING THE GUIDELINES FOR HEALTHY EATING

Six Guidelines for Healthy Eating

The six statements you read in the first activity "Rating My Eating Habits" are guidelines for healthy eating for most Americans. If you eat according to those guidelines, it doesn't mean that you will never get sick or have a heart attack later in life, but the guidelines provide the best advice for the largest number of people. Nutrition is complicated, because each person is unique and foods affect people differently. If you follow the guidelines, you are likely to get all the nutrients your body needs to be healthy without eating extra stuff that your body doesn't need. Let's look at the guidelines one at a time.

Guideline A: Eat a variety of foods each day. Your body needs more than 40 different nutrients for good health. (Nutrients are things like vitamins and minerals that your body needs to grow, to repair cuts and bruises, and to keep all of your organs working as they should.) If you eat a balanced diet with a variety of foods, you are likely to get all of the nutrients you need.

Most foods contain more than one nutrient. For example, milk provides protein, fats, sugar, riboflavin and other B vitamins, vitamin A, calcium, phosphorus, and other nutrients. Meat provides protein, several B vitamins, iron, and zinc. No single food supplies all of the nutrients in the amounts that you need. Milk, for instance, contains very little iron and meat has little calcium. So, if you eat a variety of foods, you are more likely to get all the nutrients your body needs by getting some nutrients from one kind of food and other necessary nutrients from another food.

The Food Guide Pyramid can help you select the variety of foods in the proportions that your body needs. (Remember, the guidelines are not perfect for every person, especially if someone has conditions, such as diabetes or high blood pressure. Anyone with such health conditions should talk to a doctor or a nutritionist about which guidelines to follow.) Also, notice the types of food that have the highest number of recommended servings: (1) breads, cereals, rice, and pasta; (2) vegetables; and (3) fruits. Whole-grain and enriched breads, cereals, rice, and pasta provide B vitamins, iron, protein, calories, and fiber. Fruits and vegetables are good sources of vitamin A, vitamin C, folic acid, fiber, and many minerals. (Although you need most of your foods from these three groups, not all breads, fruits, and vegetables are equally healthy. You will read more about that later.)

Guideline B: Maintain desirable weight. If you are overweight, you are more likely to develop some health problems later in your life. Obesity (the condition of being overweight or having too much body fat) can lead to high blood pressure, increased levels of cholesterol, heart disease, strokes, certain cancers, and other health problems. But, how do you know what is the right weight for you?

Because people come in very different shapes and sizes, this is a difficult question to answer. Many times, young people think that a healthy body is a thin body, but that is not necessarily the case. If you eat a balanced diet that includes lots of fruits and vegetables and you exercise regularly, you should be able to maintain a desirable weight. If you are uncertain whether your weight is desirable for you, then you should talk to a doctor or a nutritionist. That person can help you decide what is ideal for your body type and family history.

One of the worst things you can do while you are still growing is to go on a fad diet or try to lose weight too quickly. You are better off being a few pounds too heavy than to try to lose weight by some drastic means, such as by vomiting or by using laxatives. If you use those methods to stay "thin," you could end up with heart problems or even more serious health conditions. The best way to maintain a desired weight and level of body fat is to eat according to the guidelines and to exercise aerobically at least three times a week.

Guideline C: Eat foods that have complex carbohydrates and fiber, such as vegetables, fruits, and whole-grain foods. You already read about some of the benefits of this guideline from Guideline A. Whole-grain foods, vegetables, and fruits have a lot of carbohydrates, which are starches and sugars. Foods high in carbohydrates are generally good to eat because they contain half as many calories as foods high in fats, and they provide lots of vitamins, minerals, and fiber. Some foods, such as candy and other sweets, have carbohydrates, but they do not have the vitamins and minerals that your body needs. (Remember the discussion of "empty calories" from Lesson 2?)

The foods that are the healthiest for you are those that have "complex carbohydrates." Those foods, such as whole-grain breads, rice, pasta, and most vegetables, also supply the fiber that you need to avoid many problems with your digestive system, such as constipation, "irritable bowel syndrome," and other intestinal disorders. Diets low in fiber might contribute to colon cancer, although no one is sure about a direct connection.

Guideline D: Avoid foods that are high in fats. Most Americans eat too much fat in their diet. As you found out in Lesson 3, fat is not always visible on the surface of foods, such as extra fat on a piece of steak or ham. Often, fats are hidden within foods in the form of oils, butter, or margarine used in making or processing the food. Too much fat can lead to high blood pressure, heart disease, obesity, and even strokes. Based on their evidence, some scientists believe that high-fat diets are connected to breast cancer and colon cancer as well.

In following this guideline, you don't have to cut all the fat out of your diet. Some fats are necessary in your diet, but if you are like most Americans, you eat much more fat than you need. Most people need no more than 30 percent of their calories from fats, and some nutrition experts say that people would be healthier with much less than that. (You will learn more about percents and calories in the next lesson.)

Guideline E: Avoid foods that are high in sugar. You read about this guideline in Lesson 2. Too much sugar in your daily diet can lead to tooth decay and excess weight. If you eat foods that are high in sugar, you will probably not eat the foods that are high in the vitamins and minerals that your body needs.

Guideline F: Avoid foods that are high in salt, or sodium. Sodium is present in almost all processed foods. If you eat any canned foods, such as soup, vegetables, or tuna, or packaged foods, such as TV dinners or frozen pizza, you are likely to eat lots of sodium. Many sauces, pickles, snacks, sandwich meats, and fast foods have a lot of sodium. Baking soda, baking powder, and monosodium glutamate (MSG) also contain sodium. You can find sodium listed on almost every food label.

This doesn't mean that all foods that have sodium are bad for you. You need some sodium in your diet, but the foods you eat usually have much more sodium than you need. The main reason for this guideline is that extra consumption of high-sodium (high-salt) foods can lead to high blood pressure in some people. Not everyone who eats a lot of sodium will get high blood pressure, but those who have diets high in sodium are more likely to have high blood pressure. As with all the guidelines, you don't have to avoid all foods that have sodium. You should cut down mainly on those foods that have a high sodium content.

READING: GOING BEYOND THE FOOD GUIDE PYRAMID

Sometimes, it is difficult to know if you are following the guidelines. You might eat according to the number of servings listed in the Food Guide Pyramid and still be eating foods that have too much sugar, too much fat, or too many calories. As you might have noticed, the Food Guide Pyramid doesn't help you decide which foods within each category are healthy or unhealthy.

Remember the activity "Making Healthy Choices" from Lesson 3? In that activity, you chose the healthier of two foods, such as ice cream and low-fat yogurt or a hamburger and baked chicken. The first two foods would be found in the milk, yogurt, and cheese group of the Food Guide Pyramid, but low-fat yogurt is healthier for you than ice cream. The hamburger and the baked chicken are from the meat, poultry, fish, dry beans, eggs, and nuts group, but the average hamburger is higher in fat than baked chicken. Nothing in the Food Guide Pyramid helps you decide which foods within each category are healthiest to eat.

As a way to help people follow the guidelines for healthy eating, an organization called the Center for Science in the Public Interest (CSPI) designed a system of classifying foods based on how much fat, sugar, or salt (sodium) a food has. They call their system the "Healthy Eating Pyramid."

This is what the CSPI says about their Healthy Eating Pyramid:

All foods are not created equal. Some are clearly better for you than others. Yet, the U.S. Department of Agriculture's (USDA) Food Guide Pyramid puts skim milk and ice cream in the same category. Ditto for lentils and bologna, olive oil and butter, and whole wheat bread and doughnuts.

So, we've taken the USDA's pyramid (it's really a triangle!) and divided each of its food groups into "Anytime," "Sometimes," or "Seldom" foods. Now, for example, instead of just "chicken" in the meat category, you have skinless chicken drumsticks in "Anytime" and fattier skinless thighs in "Sometimes".

"Anytime" foods can be eaten at any time, just as the label suggests. You can eat as many of these foods as you like, generally as often as you like. These are the healthiest foods, such as most fruits and vegetables and whole-grain foods that are low in fat, low in sugar, and high in starches, fiber, vitamins, and minerals.

"Sometimes" foods are also reasonably healthy, but they are not as good for you as those in the "Anytime" category. Foods in this category usually have some fat, some sugar, or are made from refined grains. (Grains, such as oats, wheat, rice, and rye, are considered to be refined if they have been processed in food mills so that the brown outer covering of bran and other parts of the grain are removed. We get white flour, white rice, white noodles, white spaghetti, and white bread from refined grains. These foods still have complex carbohydrates, but they aren't as healthy as whole-grain foods like whole-wheat bread, brown rice, whole-wheat noodles, whole-wheat pizza crust, or whole-wheat flour.)

"Seldom" foods are the ones you should limit in your diet. You should eat them seldom, as the label says. The recommendation is to keep the portions of these foods small and to eat them only two or three times a week. These foods are often high in fat, high in sugar, and high in salt. They are seldom made with whole grains.

In the next activity, you will build your own Healthy Eating Pyramid using the categories of "Anytime," "Sometimes," and "Seldom" foods.

ACTIVITY: BUILDING MY OWN PYRAMID

Procedure

1. Make a data table using the categories from the Food Guide Pyramid, as follows:

FOOD CATEGORIES

Bread, Cereal, Rice, Pasta Group	Vegetable Group	Fruit Group	Milk, Yogurt, Cheese Group	Meat, Poultry, Fish, Dry Beans, Eggs, Nuts Group	Fats, Oils, Sweets, Condiments Group
1.					
2.					
3.					
4.					
5.					
6.					
7.					
8.					
9.					
10.					

2. To complete the data table, list 10 foods in each category that you like to eat or would be willing to eat.
    You might find this task easier if you work with a partner or in a team. You can share ideas, but in your data table, list only those foods that you would eat. Your list does not have to look like your partner's or teammates' lists.

3. Using An Eating Guide, on pp. 34-36 decide whether each food in your data table is an "Anytime" food, a "Sometimes" food, or a "Seldom" food. In your data table, write an "A" next to the "Anytime" foods, "SM" next to the "Sometimes" foods, and "SL" next to the "Seldom" foods.
    Again, working with others might make this task easier. If a food from your list is not in the guide, try to find foods that are similar and use the category for those foods. Think about the quality of the food. Does it have a lot of sugar? A lot of fat? Is it salty? Is it made with white or whole-wheat flour?

4. Complete the Healthy Eating Pyramid Record Page by writing the information from your data table onto the Healthy Eating Pyramid in the appropriate spaces.

5. Fill in any sections in the "Anytime" and "Sometimes" categories with foods from An Eating Guide that you would be willing to eat.
    The more choices you have in these sections, the easier it will be to follow the guidelines for healthy eating.

6. Share your personal Healthy Eating Pyramid with a partner or teammates. Discuss whether you agree with the placement of the foods in the pyramids. Change the position of those foods that you agree should be in a different category.

7. Cut out your Healthy Eating Pyramid from the Record Pages and glue the flaps so that the pyramid becomes free-standing.
    You might take your pyramid home or leave it on your desk as a reminder of which foods are "Anytime," "Sometimes," and "Seldom" foods.

WRAP UP

Make a list of all the foods you eat for the next two days. As you make your list, write an "A" next to the "Anytime" foods, "SM" next to the "Sometimes" foods, and "SL" next to the "Seldom" foods. In which category are most of the foods that you eat? Also, note whether those foods are or are not on your Healthy Eating Pyramid. If they are not, add them to your pyramid.

Write a reflection of how you feel about your eating habits. Are you satisfied with your food choices? What keeps you from eating more "Anytime" foods? What might encourage you to eat more nutritious foods? (Realize that making changes in the types of foods you eat will not happen overnight. Give yourself time to experiment with different kinds of foods and decide which healthy alternatives you like to eat. Give yourself a lot of credit if you move from eating mostly in the "Seldom" category to choosing foods from the "Sometimes" category.)

INVOLVING FAMILY MEMBERS

Take your Healthy Eating Pyramid and share it with your family members at home. After every evening meal, decide whether the foods you have just eaten are "Anytime," "Sometimes," or "Seldom" foods. Talk about changes you could make as a family so that everyone eats more "Anytime" foods and fewer "Seldom" foods.

AN EATING GUIDE

Key		
s = some sugar	f = some fat	st = some salt
S = a lot of sugar	F = a lot of fat	ST = a lot of salt
	r = refined grains	

Anytime	Sometimes	Seldom
Apple, raw	Apricot, canned in syrup (S)	Angel food cake (S)
Apple juice (unsweetened)	Avocado (f)	Bacon (F,ST)
Applesauce (unsweetened)	Bagel (f)	Beef, T-bone steak (F)
Apricot, fresh	Banana chips (S)	Beef, hamburger, regular or lean (F)
Banana	Beans, refried (f)	Bologna (F,ST)
Beans, dry, Great Northern	Beans, canned with pork (f)	Brownies (S)
Beans, green	Beef broth (ST)	Butter (F,ST)
Bean sprouts	Beef, pot roast (f)	Candy (S)
Beets	Biscuits (r)	Candy, milk chocolate (F,S)
Blackberries	Bread, white (r)	Cereal, presweetened (S)
Broccoli	Carrots, glazed (S)	Cheese, American (F,st)
Blackeyed peas	Cashews (F)	Cheese, cheddar, colby (F,st)
Bulgar	Cereals, unsweetened (r)	Cheese, cream (F)
Cabbage	Cheese, mozzarella (f)	Cheese, Swiss (F,st)
Cantaloupe	Chicken, baked/boiled with skin (f)	Chicken, commercially fried (F,ST)
Carrots	Chicken, fried at home (F)	Chocolate milk, made with whole milk (F,S)
Cauliflower	Chili, with beans & meat (f,ST)	Coconut (F)
Celery	Chocolate milk, made with skim (1%) milk (S)	Coffeecake (S)
Cereals, whole-grain	Clam chowder (f,st)	Cola (S)
Cheese, made with skim milk	Cole slaw (f)	Cookies (S,f)

Anytime	Sometimes	Seldom
Clams, steamed	Cocoa with skim milk (S)	Cupcakes (S)
Cod, baked or broiled	Cottage cheese, creamed (f)	Devils food cake (S)
Corn	Crackers, graham (S)	Doughnut (F,S)
Cottage cheese, low-fat	Crackers, saltines	Eggs, whites and yolk (F)
Egg whites	Cranberry sauce (S)	Eggnog (F,S)
Grapes	Fish, fried (f)	Fruitcake (S)
Grapefruit	Fish sticks (f)	Ham (F,ST)
Halibut	Flour tortilla (r)	Hot dogs (F,ST)
Lentils	French fries (f)	Ice cream (F,S)
Lettuce	Granola (f)	Lemonade (S)
Milk, buttermilk made from skim milk	Grapefruit juice, canned, sweetened (s)	Liver (F)
Milk, skim (1%)	Hominy grits (r)	Marshmallows (S)
Orange	Ice milk (S)	Mayonnaise (F)
Orange juice (unsweetened)	Lamb, leg, roasted (f)	Milk, whole (F)
Oatmeal	Lasagna (r,f)	Milkshake, made with whole milk (F,S)
Onions	Macaroni (r)	Mustard (ST)
Peaches, fresh	Macaroni and cheese (r,f)	Pickles (ST)
Pears, fresh	Margarine, made with vegetable oil (f,ST)	Pie (S,F)
Peas, green	Matzo (r)	Pizza, sausage or pepperoni (r,F)
Perch	Milk 2% (f)	Popcorn, caramel corn (S,F)
Pineapple, fresh	Noodles (r)	Popsicle (S)
Pineapple juice (unsweetened)	Orange juice, canned, sweetened (s)	Potato chips (F,ST)
Popcorn, air popped, no salt or butter	Pancakes with syrup (r,S)	Root beer (S)
Potatoes, baked or boiled	Peanuts (f,ST)	Salad dressing (F)
Rice, brown	Peanut butter (F)	Salami (F,ST)

35

Anytime	Sometimes	Seldom
Shredded wheat	Pears, canned in syrup (S)	Sauerkraut (ST)
Sole	Pizza, cheese (r,f)	Sausage (F,ST)
Spinach	Pizza, vegetarian (r,f)	Spareribs (F)
Sprouts	Popcorn, no butter (st,f)	Tomato ketchup (s,ST)
Squash	Pork, shoulder or loin , lean (f)	Yogurt, made with whole milk, sweetened , (F,S)
Strawberries	Potato salad (f)	
Sweet potatoes, no glaze	Prunes (S)	
Tomatoes	Raisins (S)	
Tuna fish, canned in water	Rice, white (r)	
Turkey, roasted without skin	Round steak (f)	
Vegetables, mixed	Rump roast (f)	
Watermelon	Salmon, canned (ST)	
Yogurt, low-fat, plain	Scallops (f)	
	Shrimp (f)	
	Sirloin steak, lean (f)	
	Spaghetti (r)	
	Spaghetti with meat sauce (f,r)	
	Soup, canned (ST)	
	Sunflower seeds (f,st)	
	Sweet potatoes with glaze (S)	
	Tofu (f)	
	Tuna, canned in oil (f)	
	Turkey, roasted with skin (f)	
	Veal (f)	
	Waffles with syrup (r,S)	
	Walnuts (f)	
	Yogurt, low-fat, sweetened (S)	

Source: "New American Eating Guide," Center for Science in the Public Interest, Washington, D.C.

UNDERSTANDING THE NUTRITION FACTS

Hey, what's for breakfast? How about a bowl of Bucko's, the cereal for serious cowpokes everywhere! Whoa, you say.... You've got to check the label and get the Nutrition Facts? Well, partner, if you insist, I guess we'll give it a whirl. But, just what do all these numbers mean?

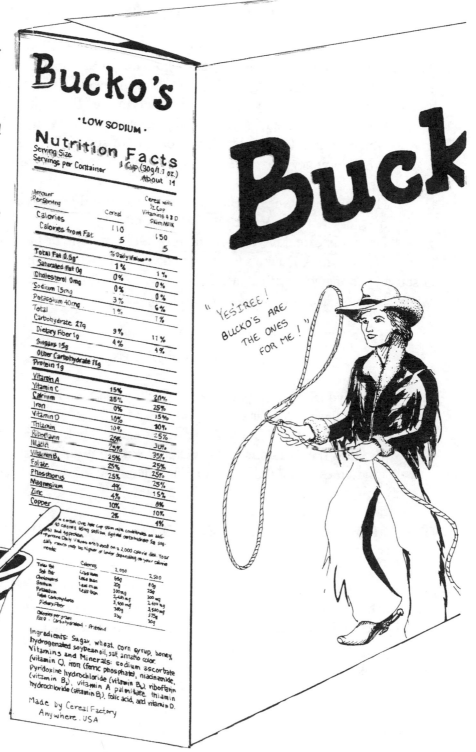

Bucko's
· LOW SODIUM ·

Nutrition Facts
Serving Size 1 Cup (30g/1.1 oz.)
Servings per Container About 14

Amount Per Serving	Cereal	Cereal with ½ Cup Vitamins A & D Skim Milk
Calories	110	150
Calories from Fat	5	5

	% Daily Value**	
Total Fat 0.5g*	1%	1%
Saturated Fat 0g	0%	0%
Cholesterol 0mg	0%	0%
Sodium 15mg	3%	6%
Potassium 40mg	1%	7%
Total Carbohydrate 27g	9%	11%
Dietary Fiber 1g	4%	4%
Sugars 15g		
Other Carbohydrate 11g		
Protein 1g		
Vitamin A	15%	20%
Vitamin C	25%	25%
Calcium	0%	15%
Iron	10%	10%
Vitamin D	10%	10%
Thiamin	25%	25%
Riboflavin	25%	30%
Niacin	25%	35%
Vitamin B6	25%	25%
Folate	25%	25%
Phosphorus	4%	25%
Magnesium	4%	15%
Zinc	10%	8%
Copper	2%	4%

* Amount in cereal. One half cup skim milk contributes an additional 40 calories, 65mg sodium, 6g total carbohydrate (6g sugars) and 4g protein.
** Percent Daily Values are based on a 2,000 calorie diet. Your daily values may be higher or lower depending on your calorie needs:

	Calories	2,000	2,500
Total Fat	Less than	65g	80g
Sat Fat	Less than	20g	25g
Cholesterol	Less than	300mg	300mg
Sodium	Less than	2,400mg	2,400mg
Potassium		3,500mg	3,500mg
Total Carbohydrate		300g	375g
Dietary Fiber		25g	30g

Calories per gram:
Fat 9 · Carbohydrate 4 · Protein 4

Ingredients: Sugar, wheat, corn syrup, honey, hydrogenated soybean oil, salt, annatto color. Vitamins and Minerals: sodium ascorbate (vitamin C), iron (ferric phosphate), niacinamide, pyridoxine hydrochloride (vitamin B6), riboflavin (vitamin B2), vitamin A palmitate, thiamin hydrochloride (vitamin B1), folic acid, and vitamin D.

Made by Cereal Factory
Anywhere, USA

" YES'IREE! BUCKO'S ARE THE ONES FOR ME ! "

Buck

ACTIVITY: WHAT DO ALL THESE NUMBERS MEAN?

Procedure

1. Read the Nutrition Facts on the side panel of Bucko's Cereal.
   This panel is the "food label" and provides important information about what the food contains.

2. Using information from the Nutrition Facts, answer the following questions:
   Write your answers on a separate piece of paper.
   a. If you ate two servings of Bucko's, how many cups of cereal would you eat?
   b. How many calories would be in two servings of Bucko's without milk? with milk?
   c. How many grams of sugar would you eat in two servings of Bucko's?
   d. Do you think that is a little sugar or a lot of sugar?
   e. Would you get more fiber or sugar if you ate two servings of Bucko's? How much more?
   f. How many servings of Bucko's with milk would you have to eat to get 100 percent of your "% Daily Value" for carbohydrates?
   g. Does this cereal have more carbohydrates, protein, or fats? How do you know?
   h. Do you think Bucko's is a nutritious cereal? Why or why not?

3. Discuss your answers with a partner.
   If your answers are not the same, discuss the differences and try to agree on one answer.

Stop and Discuss

1. Share your answers with your classmates and teacher. Note the questions where classmates disagree.
2. What does the "% Daily Value" tell you about eating this food?
3. Review the Guidelines for Healthy Eating from Lesson 5. For which guidelines could the Nutrition Facts help you make good decisions?

ACTIVITY: MAKING HEALTHY DECISIONS ABOUT NUTRITION

Procedure

1. Read each situation that follows. Decide which food choice would make a healthy decision.
2. Write your decision and explain what helped you make that decision.
3. Discuss your choices with your classmates. What information from the Nutrition Facts helped you make your decision?

Situation 1:

John read in a magazine that most Americans eat too much sugar and not enough fiber. He read that fiber helps prevent some stomach problems and might help prevent some types of cancer. He wants to eat a cereal that is low in sugar and high in fiber. Which cereal should John choose?

Cereal 1 (Cheerios)

Nutrition Facts

Serving Size 1 cup (30g)
Servings Per Container About 14

Amount Per Serving	Cheerios	with ½ cup skim milk
Calories	110	150
Calories from Fat	15	20
	% Daily Value**	
Total Fat 2g*	3%	3%
Saturated Fat 0g	0%	2%
Cholesterol 0mg	0%	1%
Sodium 280mg	12%	14%
Potassium 90mg	3%	8%
Total Carbohydrate 23g	8%	10%
Dietary Fiber 3g	11%	11%
Sugars 1g		
Other Carbohydrate 19g		
Protein 3g		
Vitamin A	25%	30%
Vitamin C	25%	25%
Calcium	4%	20%
Iron	45%	45%
Vitamin D	10%	25%
Thiamin	25%	30%
Riboflavin	25%	35%
Niacin	25%	25%
Vitamin B₆	25%	25%
Folic Acid	25%	25%
Phosphorus	10%	25%
Magnesium	8%	10%
Zinc	25%	30%
Copper	4%	4%

*Amount in Cereal. A serving of cereal plus skim milk provides 2g fat (0.5g saturated fat), less than 5mg cholesterol, 350mg sodium, 290mg potassium, 29g carbohydrate (7g sugars) and 7g protein.

**Percent Daily Values are based on a 2,000 calorie diet. Your daily values may be higher or lower depending on your calorie needs:

	Calories:	2,000	2,500
Total Fat	Less than	65g	80g
Sat Fat	Less than	20g	25g
Cholesterol	Less than	300mg	300mg
Sodium	Less than	2,400mg	2,400mg
Potassium		3,500mg	3,500mg
Total Carbohydrate		300g	375g
Dietary Fiber		25g	30g

INGREDIENTS: WHOLE OAT FLOUR (INCLUDES THE OAT BRAN), MODIFIED FOOD STARCH, WHEAT STARCH, SUGAR, SALT, OAT FIBER, TRISODIUM PHOSPHATE, CALCIUM CARBONATE. VITAMIN E (MIXED TOCOPHEROLS) ADDED TO PRESERVE FRESHNESS.

Cereal 2

Nutrition Facts

Serving Size 1 cup (49g)
Servings Per Container about 10

Amount Per Serving	Cereal	Cereal with ½ cup Skim Milk
Calories	170	210
Calories from Fat	5	5
	% Daily Value**	
Total Fat 0.5g*	1%	1%
Saturated Fat 0g	0%	0%
Polyunsaturated Fat 0g		
Monounsaturated Fat 0g		
Cholesterol 0mg	0%	0%
Sodium 0mg	0%	3%
Potassium 200mg	6%	11%
Total Carbohydrate 41g	14%	16%
Dietary Fiber 5g	21%	21%
Insoluble Fiber 5g		
Sugars 0g		
Other Carbohydrate 36g		
Protein 5g		
Vitamin A	0%	4%
Vitamin C	0%	2%
Calcium	2%	15%
Iron	8%	8%
Vitamin D	0%	15%
Thiamin	8%	10%
Riboflavin	2%	10%
Niacin	15%	15%
Phosphorus	20%	30%
Magnesium	15%	20%
Zinc	8%	10%
Copper	8%	8%

*Amount in Cereal. One half cup skim milk contributes an additional 40 calories, 65mg sodium, 200mg potassium, 6g total carbohydrate (6g sugars), and 4g protein.

**Percent Daily Values are based on a 2,000 calorie diet. Your daily values may be higher or lower depending on your calorie needs:

	Calories:	2,000	2,500
Total Fat	Less than	65g	80g
Saturated Fat	Less than	20g	25g
Cholesterol	Less than	300mg	300mg
Sodium	Less than	2,400mg	2,400mg
Potassium		3,500mg	3,500mg
Total Carbohydrate		300g	375g
Dietary Fiber		25g	30g

INGREDIENTS: WHOLE WHEAT. TO PRESERVE THE NATURAL WHEAT FLAVOR, BHT IS ADDED TO THE PACKAGING MATERIAL.

Cereal 3

Nutrition Facts

Serving Size 1 cup (56g)
Servings Per Container about 8

Amount Per Serving	Cereal Alone	with 1/2 Cup Vitamin A&D Fortified Skim Milk
Calories	220	260
Calories from Fat	25	25
	% Daily Value**	
Total Fat 2.5g*	4%	4%
Saturated Fat 0.5g	2%	2%
Polyunsaturated Fat 1g		
Monounsaturated Fat 1g		
Cholesterol 0mg	0%	0%
Sodium 260mg	11%	14%
Potassium 230mg	7%	12%
Total Carbohydrate 43g	14%	16%
Other Carbohydrate 30g		
Dietary Fiber 4g	17%	17%
Soluble Fiber 2g		
Insol Fiber 2g		
Sugars 9g		
Protein 7g		
Vitamin A	10%	15%
Vitamin C	10%	10%
Calcium	2%	15%
Iron	80%	80%
Vitamin E	10%	10%
Thiamin	25%	30%
Riboflavin	25%	35%
Niacin	25%	25%
Vitamin B₆	25%	30%
Folate	25%	25%
Zinc	25%	30%

*Amount in Cereal. One half cup skim milk contributes an additional 40 Calories, 65mg Sodium, 6g Total Carbohydrate (6g Sugars), and 4g Protein.

**Percent Daily Values are based on a 2,000 calorie diet. Your daily values may be higher or lower depending on your calorie needs:

	Calories:	2,000	2,500
Total Fat	Less than	65g	80g
Sat Fat	Less than	20g	25g
Cholesterol	Less than	300mg	300mg
Sodium	Less than	2,400mg	2,400mg
Total Carbohydrate		300g	375g
Dietary Fiber		25g	30g
Potassium		3,500mg	3,500mg

Calories per gram:
Fat 9 • Carbohydrate 4 • Protein 4

Ingredients: Whole oat flour (with oat bran), whole wheat flour, sugar, maltodextrin, malted barley extract, molasses, brown sugar, baking soda, salt.

Situation 2:

Maria wants to lose weight. Which kind of milk would be best for her to drink?

GRADE A PASTEURIZED

Nutrition Facts	
Serving Size 1 cup (236mL)	
Servings Per Container 2	

Amount Per Serving	
Calories 90	Calories from Fat 0

	% Daily Value*
Total Fat 0g	**0%**
Saturated Fat 0g	**0%**
Cholesterol 5mg	**1%**
Sodium 130mg	**5%**
Total Carbohydrate 13g	**4%**
Dietary Fiber 0g	**0%**
Sugars 12g	
Protein 9g	**17%**

Vitamin A 10% • Vitamin C 4%
Calcium 30% • Iron 0% • Vitamin D 25%

*Percent Daily Values are based on a 2,000 calorie diet. Your daily values may be higher or lower depending on your calorie needs:

		Calories	2,000	2,500
Total Fat	Less than		65g	80g
Sat. Fat	Less than		20g	25g
Cholesterol	Less than		300mg	300mg
Sodium	Less than		2,400mg	2,400mg
Total Carbohydrate			300g	375g
Dietary Fiber			25g	30g
Protein			50g	65g

**GRADE A
PASTEURIZED, HOMOGENIZED**

Nutrition Facts	
Serving Size 1 cup (236mL)	
Servings Per Container 2	

Amount Per Serving	
Calories 130	Calories from Fat 45

	% Daily Value*
Total Fat 5g	**8%**
Saturated Fat 3g	**15%**
Cholesterol 20mg	**7%**
Sodium 125mg	**5%**
Total Carbohydrate 13g	**4%**
Dietary Fiber 0g	**0%**
Sugars 12g	
Protein 8g	**17%**

Vitamin A 10% • Vitamin C 4%
Calcium 30% • Iron 0% • Vitamin D 25%

*Percent Daily Values are based on a 2,000 calorie diet. Your daily values may be higher or lower depending on your calorie needs:

		Calories	2,000	2,500
Total Fat	Less than		65g	80g
Sat. Fat	Less than		20g	25g
Cholesterol	Less than		300mg	300mg
Sodium	Less than		2,400mg	2,400mg
Total Carbohydrate			300g	375g
Dietary Fiber			25g	30g
Protein			50g	65g

**GRADE A
PASTEURIZED, HOMOGENIZED**

Nutrition Facts	
Serving Size 1 cup (236mL)	
Servings Per Container 2	

Amount Per Serving	
Calories 160	Calories from Fat 70

	% Daily Value*
Total Fat 8g	**12%**
Saturated Fat 5g	**25%**
Cholesterol 35mg	**11%**
Sodium 125mg	**5%**
Total Carbohydrate 13g	**4%**
Dietary Fiber 0g	**0%**
Sugars 12g	
Protein 8g	**17%**

Vitamin A 6% • Vitamin C 4%
Calcium 30% • Iron 0% • Vitamin D 25%

*Percent Daily Values are based on a 2,000 calorie diet. Your daily values may be higher or lower depending on your calorie needs:

		Calories	2,000	2,500
Total Fat	Less than		65g	80g
Sat. Fat	Less than		20g	25g
Cholesterol	Less than		300mg	300mg
Sodium	Less than		2,400mg	2,400mg
Total Carbohydrate			300g	375g
Dietary Fiber			25g	30g
Protein			50g	65g

Situation 3:

Manuel saw a program on television that linked high-fat foods with heart disease. He doesn't want to have heart disease when he gets older. Which snack would be healthiest for him to eat?

Nutrition Facts
Serving Size 1 Container (227g)

Amount Per Serving

Calories 240   Calories from Fat 25

	% Daily Value*
Total Fat 3g	**5%**
Saturated Fat 1.5g	**8%**
Cholesterol 15mg	**5%**
Sodium 135mg	**6%**
Potassium 470mg	**13%**
Total Carbohydrate 46g	**15%**
Dietary Fiber 1g	**4%**
Sugars 44g	
Protein 9g	

Vitamin A 2% • Vitamin C 20%
Calcium 35% • Iron 0%

*Percent Daily Values are based on a 2,000 calorie diet.

INGREDIENTS: GRADE A LOWFAT MILK, STRAWBERRIES, SUGAR, HIGH FRUCTOSE CORN SYRUP, NATURAL FLAVORS, PECTIN, BEET JUICE (FOR COLOR), AND YOGURT CULTURES WITH *L. ACIDOPHILUS.*

Nutrition Facts
Serving Size 1 oz. (28g/About 17 chips)
Servings Per Container 6

Amount Per Serving

Calories 160   Calories from Fat 90

	% Daily Value*
Total Fat 10g	**16%**
Saturated Fat 3g	**15%**
Cholesterol 0mg	**0%**
Sodium 180mg	**8%**
Total Carbohydrate 14g	**5%**
Dietary Fiber 1g	**5%**
Sugars 0g	
Protein 2g	

Vitamin A 0% • Vitamin C 10%
Calcium 0% • Iron 0%

° Percent Daily Values are based on a 2,000 calorie diet. Your daily values may be higher or lower depending on your calorie needs:

	Calories:	2,000	2,500
Total Fat	Less than	65g	80g
Sat Fat	Less than	20g	25g
Cholesterol	Less than	300mg	300mg
Sodium	Less than	2,400mg	2,400mg
Total Carbohydrate		300g	375g
Dietary Fiber		25g	30g

Calories per gram:
Fat 9 • Carbohydrate 4 • Protein 4

Ingredients: Potatoes, Vegetable Oil (Contains one or more of the following: Canola, Corn, Cottonseed, or Partially Hydrogenated [Canola, Soybean, or Sunflower] Oil), and Salt.

No Preservatives.

Nutrition Facts
Serving Size 18 Crackers (29g)
Servings Per Container About 9

Amount Per Serving

Calories 120   Calories from Fat 35

	% Daily Value*
Total Fat 4g	**6%**
Saturated Fat 0.5g	**3%**
Polyunsaturated Fat 0g	
Monounsaturated Fat 1.5g	
Cholesterol 0mg	**0%**
Sodium 220mg	**9%**
Total Carbohydrate 21g	**7%**
Dietary Fiber 2g	**7%**
Sugars 3g	
Protein 2g	

Vitamin A 0% • Vitamin C 0%
Calcium 2% • Iron 4% • Phosphorus 10%

* Percent Daily Values are based on a 2,000 calorie diet. Your daily values may be higher or lower depending on your calorie needs:

	Calories:	2,000	2,500
Total Fat	Less than	65g	80g
Sat Fat	Less than	20g	25g
Cholesterol	Less than	300mg	300mg
Sodium	Less than	2,400mg	2,400mg
Total Carbohydrate		300g	375g
Dietary Fiber		25g	30g

INGREDIENTS: WHOLE WHEAT FLOUR, ENRICHED WHEAT FLOUR (CONTAINS NIACIN, REDUCED IRON, THIAMINE MONONITRATE [VITAMIN B₁], RIBOFLAVIN [VITAMIN B₂]), VEGETABLE SHORTENING (PARTIALLY HYDROGENATED SOYBEAN OIL), SUGAR, SALT, HIGH FRUCTOSE CORN SYRUP, MALTED BARLEY FLOUR, LEAVENING (CALCIUM PHOSPHATE, BAKING SODA), ANNATTO EXTRACT AND TURMERIC OLEORESIN (VEGETABLE COLORS).

BHT IS ADDED TO THE PACKAGING MATERIAL TO HELP PRESERVE PRODUCT FRESHNESS.

Nutrition Facts
Serving Size 1 snack (113g)
Servings Per Container 6

Calories 160
Calories from Fat 45

Amount/Serving	% Daily Value*	Amount/Serving	% Daily Value*
Total Fat 5g	8%	**Total Carbohydrate** 28g	9%
Saturated Fat 2g	9%	Dietary Fiber 0g	0%
Cholesterol 0mg	0%	Sugars 23g	
Sodium 190mg	8%	**Protein** 3g	

Vitamin A 2% • Vitamin C 0% • Calcium 10% • Iron 6%

*Percent Daily Values are based on a 2,000 calorie diet. Your daily values may be higher or lower depending on your calorie needs:

	Calories:	2,000	2,500
Total Fat	Less than	65g	80g
Sat Fat	Less than	20g	25g
Cholest	Less than	300mg	300mg
Sodium	Less than	2,400mg	2,400mg
Total Carb		300g	375g
Fiber		25g	30g

INGREDIENTS: SKIM MILK, SUGAR, PARTIALLY HYDROGENATED COTTONSEED OIL, CORNSTARCH MODIFIED, COCOA PROCESSED WITH ALKALI, SALT, SODIUM STEAROYL LACTYLATE (FOR SMOOTH TEXTURE), NATURAL AND ARTIFICIAL FLAVOR.

• No Preservatives

966501AR6P

WRAP UP

Bring to class food labels (Nutrition Facts) from a variety of foods. Compare similar types of food for fat content, sugar content, sodium (salt) content, and fiber. Decide which foods are healthy or unhealthy choices based on the information in the labels. Organize the labels in order from those with the least fat to those with the most fat, or from those with the least sugar to those with the most sugar. Were you surprised by any of the information you learned from reading the Nutrition Facts?

Look at the charts of healthy and unhealthy foods you made in Lesson 1. Do you think you should change any of the foods from healthy to unhealthy (or vice versa) because of what you learned by reading the Nutrition Facts on food labels? Which foods are not as healthy as you thought they were? Which foods are healthier than you thought they were?

INVOLVING FAMILY MEMBERS

Explain to family members what you have learned about reading food labels. Then, accompany your parents or guardians to the grocery store and look for foods that will help your family meet the Guidelines for Healthy Eating, such as "eat foods that have complex carbohydrates and fiber, such as vegetables, fruits, and whole-grain foods"; "avoid foods that are high in fats"; "avoid foods that are high in sugar"; and "avoid foods that are high in salt, or sodium." Compare the Nutrition Facts of the foods you might select, and point out the places in the Nutrition Facts that will help your family members make healthier decisions about the foods they eat.

IT'S IN THE CARDS!

Can healthy eating be fun? Try the Healthy Meals Card Game and find out!

Healthy Meals Card Game
--a game for three to four players--

Object of the Game

    The object of this game is to create a complete, healthy meal from foods shown on the cards. To be complete, each meal must have a main dish, a side dish, a vegetable, a beverage, and a dessert. To be healthy, each meal must be mainly from the Anytime and Sometimes foods listed in An Eating Guide. (See Lesson 5.) Because a person should have only a few Seldom foods each week, no more than one Seldom food can be part of the meal.

    The cards show whether the food is a main dish, a side dish, a vegetable, a beverage, or a dessert. You have to decide which food is an "Anytime" food, a "Sometimes" food, or a "Seldom" food.

ACTIVITY: PLAYING THE HEALTHY MEALS CARD GAME

Procedure

1.   Find two or three partners with whom to play the game.
2.   Choose one person to begin as the dealer and one person to be the scorekeeper.
     The scorekeeper should have pencil and paper.
3.   The dealer shuffles the cards; deals them face down, one at a time, until each player has five cards; places the remainder of the cards face down in the center of the playing area; and turns the top card over and lays it face up next to the deck of cards.
     The "face-up" cards will become the discard pile.
4.   Play the game as follows:
     a.   The person to the right of the dealer begins play either by taking the top card from the face-down pile or by taking the top card form the discard pile.
     b.   The player either keeps the new card and discards another from his or her hand, or the player may discard the new card.
          For each turn, a player must take one card and discard one card.
     c.   Players take turns drawing and discarding until one player says, "I have a healthy meal."
          To say, "I have a healthy meal," a player must have the following in his or her hand:
          a main dish
          a side dish
          a vegetable
          a beverage
          a dessert
          no more than one "Seldom" food
     d.   When a player calls, "I have a healthy meal," that player must show his or her cards to prove that the cards show a complete, healthy meal.
          All players must agree that the hand contains only one "Seldom" food and all five categories for a complete meal. If the cards show a healthy meal, then play stops for that hand.
     e.   The scorekeeper then tallies each person's score.
          See "How to Score the Game."
     f.   The person to the right of the dealer becomes the new dealer for the next hand of the game.
     g.   The winner of the game is the first player to score 40 points.

How to Score the Game

When play stops, all players must show their cards. All players must agree on which foods are "Anytime," "Sometimes," and "Seldom" foods in each player's hand. The team may refer to An Eating Guide from Lesson 5 to help them decide on the categories.

Every "Anytime" card is worth 2 points.
Every "Sometimes" card is worth 1 point.

For every "Seldom" card, the player loses 1 point.

The player who calls "I have a healthy meal" gets 2 bonus points if he or she has a healthy meal. The player who calls "I have a healthy meal" loses 1 point if the meal is not a healthy one.

Stop and Discuss

1. How would you describe a healthy meal?
2. Broccoli is an "Anytime" food. Why is broccoli with cheese sauce a "Sometimes" food?
3. Why is skim milk considered a healthier choice than either 2% or whole milk?
4. What did you learn about healthy eating from playing this card game?
5. Is this card game related to "real life"? If so, how?

WRAP UP

Play the Healthy Meals Card Game with younger students. Decide whether you should make new cards and label the pictures as "Anytime," "Sometimes," and "Seldom" foods. Decide how you would introduce the game to the younger students. Would you have to tell them something about healthy eating before beginning the game or could they learn about healthy eating by playing the game?

INVOLVING FAMILY MEMBERS

Take a set of the cards home and play the Healthy Meals Card Game with your family. Do your family members agree or disagree about which foods are "Anytime," "Sometimes," or "Seldom" foods? If you cannot agree, how could you use the Nutrition Facts on food labels to help you reach an agreement?

WHAT ABOUT FAST FOODS?

On a piece of scrap paper, write what you usually eat when you go to a fast-food restaurant. Now, review the Guidelines for Healthy Eating:

Eat a variety of foods each day.
Maintain desirable weight.
Eat foods that have complex carbohydrates and fiber, such as vegetables, fruits, and whole-grain foods.
Avoid foods that are high in fats.
Avoid foods that are high in sugar.
Avoid foods that are high in salt, or sodium.

Does your favorite fast-food meal meet these guidelines? Why or why not? To meet the guidelines, would you change what you eat in a fast-food restaurant? Why or why not?

In this lesson, you will look at some fast-food menus and decide how you can make healthier choices, even at your favorite restaurants.

ACTIVITY: EATING ON THE RUN

Most Americans eat at least two meals a week in a fast-food restaurant. In fact, many young people would rather eat at a fast-food restaurant than anywhere else. In this activity, you will analyze some of the choices available from the menus of selected fast-food restaurants. Your task will be to choose meals from those menus that best meet the guidelines for healthy eating.

Procedure

1. Meet with a partner or become a member of a team.
    Your teacher might assign the partners or teams, or you might select your own. Follow your teacher's directions.
2. Write your team's assignment of a fast-food restaurant.
    Your team might be asked to select a restaurant, or your teacher might assign one for you. Not every team can select the same restaurant because each restaurant must be analyzed by at least one team.
3. Make the following data table on a separate piece of paper.
    Each team member does not need a separate data table; you need one data table for your team. Your team will analyze the menu from one fast-food restaurant using the following four guidelines.
    > *Maintain desirable weight.*
    > *Avoid foods that are high in fats.*
    > *Avoid foods that are high in sugar.*
    > *Avoid foods that are high in salt, or sodium.*

Fast-Foods Data Table

Name of Fast-Food Restaurant:

Name of Food	Calories	Fat (in grams)	% Daily Value	Sugar (in grams)	Sodium (in milligrams)	% Daily Value

4. Using the menu from your fast-food restaurant, list the foods in order from the one with the highest number of calories to the one with the lowest number of calories.
    Your teacher will provide the restaurant menu your team will analyze.

5. Complete the remainder of the table by filling in the number of grams of fat, sugar, and sodium for each food listed.

6. Using the information from your data table, decide which foods you would select to make a complete, nutritious meal at this restaurant. Write your selections on a separate piece of paper and include the information about calories, grams of fat and sugar, and milligrams of sodium for each food.
    A complete meal can include a main dish, a side dish, a beverage, and a dessert, or you can choose only a main dish and a beverage. To be nutritious, the meal must meet as many of the guidelines for healthy eating as possible. Use the data on calories to help with the guideline for maintaining desirable weight. If you consume extra calories, you are more likely to gain weight.

7. Be prepared to explain why you selected the foods that you did and to explain which guidelines you used to help you select the most nutritious foods.

8. Review the selected meal in a class discussion.

Stop and Discuss

1. What did you learn about the different fast-food restaurants and their food choices?

2. Would you classify the food choices as "Anytime," "Sometimes," or "Seldom" foods? Why?

3. At which restaurant(s) do you think you could eat the healthiest meals? Why?

4. Would you be willing to change the foods you eat at fast-food restaurants? Why or why not?

5. Can you still eat your favorite foods at fast-food restaurants and follow the Guidelines for Healthy Eating?

WRAP UP

The new food labels state that people should base their diets on the following numbers:

Calories   2,000 calories per day
             (This is the guideline for most people; however, people who
             are very active and many teenage boys can eat 2,500 calories
             per day and not gain excess weight.)

Fat   Less than 65 grams (g) per day

Sugars	Less than 50 grams (g) per day
	(This information is not on the food label, but some nutritionists recommend 50 grams per day as a reasonable guideline.)
Cholesterol	Less than 300 milligrams (mg) per day
Sodium	Less than 2,400 milligrams (mg) per day
Fiber	At least 25 grams (g) per day

Working with your partner or team and using your Fast-Food Data Table or fast-food restaurant menu, answer the following questions about the meal you selected in Step 6 in the activity "Eating on the Run." (To look at the amounts of cholesterol and fiber, you will need to go back to the restaurant menu.)

1. If you ate this meal, how many more calories, grams of fat, and milligrams of sodium could you eat the rest of the day and stay within the guidelines?
2. What percent of your daily allowance for fat grams would this meal provide?
3. What percent of your daily allowance for cholesterol would this meal provide?
4. What percent of your daily allowance for fiber would this meal provide?
5. Do you think this meal is high or low in the categories listed above? (Keep in mind that one meal is about 1/4 to 1/3 of the food you eat each day, depending on how many meals and snacks you eat each day.)
6. Given this information, do you think that you usually eat within the food label guidelines? Why or why not?

INVOLVING FAMILY MEMBERS

The next time your family goes to eat at a fast-food restaurant, ask a restaurant manager for the nutritional information about the foods they serve at the restaurant. (Many fast-food restaurants have that information available or can give you an address for obtaining the information.) Compare the number of calories and the amounts of fat, cholesterol, sugar, fiber, and sodium of the food choices at the different fast-food restaurants. Decide which fast-food restaurants give your family the most nutritious choices. If your favorite fast-food restaurant does not provide the most nutritious choices, suggest some foods that would make the choices more nutritious. (Suggest foods that you think most people would like to eat and that you would be willing to buy at the restaurant.)

LESSON 9

TELEVISION AD-VENTURES

Television is a powerful force in our society. Some say that television influences what we wear, how we talk, what we buy, and if we would react violently in certain situations. Do you think that television programs and commercials persuade people to eat certain foods? Do you think children under 12, teenagers, or adults would be the group most influenced by television ads to eat certain foods? Why do you think so?

In this lesson, you will watch and listen to television advertisements about food products. As you watch and listen, think about the questions above. How much influence do you think television ads have on you and your family's food choices?

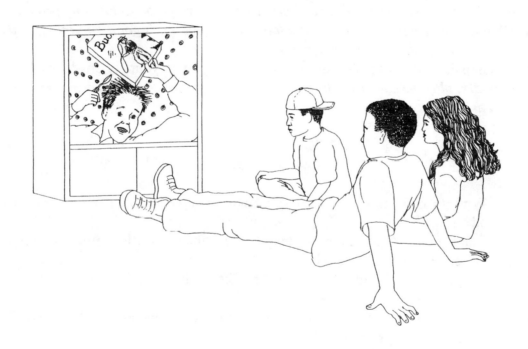

ACTIVITY: WE'LL BE RIGHT BACK AFTER A WORD FROM OUR SPONSORS

In this activity, you will watch a series of television commercials that advertise food products. As you watch the commercials, think carefully about the messages in the ad.

51

Procedure

1.   On a separate piece of paper, construct the following data table:

Television Advertisements
Data Table

Food Product Advertised	Reasons Given To Buy This Product

2.   Watch and listen carefully to each commercial that your teacher shows.

3.   After each commercial, complete one row in the data table.
Write all the reasons that the advertisers use to convince you to buy this product. Some possibilities include the following: The food tastes good. It is good for you. It is part of a nutritious breakfast. You can win prizes.

4.   After completing the data table, discuss your findings with your classmates and teacher.
If necessary, play the commercials a second time and pause the tape each time you hear or see a reason to buy this product.

Stop and Discuss

1.   Why do companies use television, radio, magazines, and newspapers to advertise their products?

2.   Using your data table, what technique do you think advertisers use most often to get people to buy a food product?

3.   Do you think the advertisements are effective in convincing people to buy certain foods? Why or why not?

4.   Would you classify the food products in these commercials as "Anytime," "Sometimes," or "Seldom" foods?

5.   Would you buy any of the foods you saw advertised in these commercials? Why or why not?

ACTIVITY: A SURVEY OF TELEVISION ADS

In this activity, you will choose a time to watch television and will collect information about the advertisements shown during that time. Then, you will analyze your information in class and draw some conclusions about advertisements for food products.

Procedure

1. On a separate piece of paper, construct the following data table:

Home Television Survey
Data Table

Day and Time	Name of Food Product Advertised	Type of Food ("Anytime," "Sometimes," "Seldom")	Who is the Target Audience? (children, teenagers, adults, whole family)	Reasons Given in the Ad for Buying Product	Would You Buy This Product? Why or why not?

2. Form teams of three or four. With your teammates, decide on the day and time of day that each of you will complete the survey. Record your selected day and time in the first column of the data table.
    Each teammate should select a different day and time. For example, one might select Saturday morning from 9:00-10:00 a.m. and another might select Wednesday evening from 6:30-7:30 p.m. Follow any guidelines that your family has for viewing television. If you are not allowed to watch television, you might look for food advertisements in the newspaper or in magazines.

3. Review the data table with your classmates and teacher.
    Be sure everyone understands how to complete the data table.

4. Take your data table home. Complete the data table as you watch the commercials during the time you selected.
    Because this is a homework assignment, you should discuss the purpose of the survey with your family members and ask them not to disturb you during the commercial breaks. You might encourage family members to help you with your assignment.

5. Bring your completed data table to class and share the information with your teammates. Discuss any similarities or differences in your data.

WRAP UP

With your teammates, design a television commercial or a magazine advertisement for an "Anytime" food. Decide which food to advertise, who is the intended audience, and when you should advertise this particular food product. Think about the advertisements you watched. What made some ads more effective than others? What might convince someone to eat this food?

Present your advertisement or commercial before the class. Discuss the different ads presented. Which were most effective? Why?

INVOLVING FAMILY MEMBERS

Becoming a wise consumer is important. You can help yourself and your family members become wiser consumers by discussing the ways advertisements influence your lives. Involve your family members in the take-home activity "A Survey of Television Ads." As you watch the commercials, discuss their reactions to the ads. Who would be convinced to buy this food product? Why would they buy it? Notice whether the ads appeal more to children or to adults. Discuss whether the foods advertised are healthy or not.

Continue to study the advertisements for food products when you watch television. Do the ads change with different types of programs? Are the ads during children's shows different from those aired during "prime time"? What techniques do advertisers use to convince you to buy their products? Do you think the ads help your family make healthier choices about the foods you eat?

LESSON 10

LET'S EAT!

You have learned a lot about nutrition in this unit. You know how to find added sugar from lists of ingredients. You know how to read Nutrition Facts and identify foods that are high in fat or cholesterol. You know about "Anytime," "Sometimes," and "Seldom" foods and which to choose for a healthy diet. And, you know six guidelines for healthy eating. That's more than a lot of adults know about nutrition!

It's time to find out if you can put all that information to work for you in choosing what you eat every day. How can you eat better to stay healthy? The best way is to plan and apply what you know about healthy eating. By eating nutritious foods and getting plenty of exercise, you might prevent many diseases in the future and feel great every day.

ACTIVITY: PLANNING HEALTHY MEALS

Procedure

1.   Locate a copy of An Eating Guide and your Healthy Eating Pyramid from Lesson 5.
      *You could use the food labels from Lesson 6, or bring in additional food labels from foods
      you like to eat.*

2. Construct two of the following menu planning data tables:

Healthy Meals Data Table

Meal	Foods Selected	Category of Food ("Anytime," "Sometimes," "Seldom")	Notes About the Food
Breakfast			
Lunch			
Dinner			
Snacks			

3. Complete the first column in the two data tables by listing foods that would be healthy choices for you and your family members for each meal and snacks.
   Working with a partner or in a team might make this step more fun. Try to follow the Guidelines for Healthy Eating by selecting a variety of foods and including foods that are low in fats, added sugar, and sodium. Remember to choose no more than two "seldom" foods each day.

4. To check your food choices, complete the next two columns of the data tables by classifying the foods as "Anytime," "Sometimes," or "Seldom" foods and by writing notes about each food, such as "low in fat," "has some added sugar," or "is a whole-grain food."
   Use An Eating Guide, your Healthy Eating Pyramid, or Nutrition Facts from food labels to help you classify the selected foods.

5. If you feel you have selected too many "seldom" foods or not enough "anytime" foods, make changes in your food lists for healthier choices.

6.   Share your Healthy Meals Data Tables with other students. Add to your data tables any new ideas of healthy foods you think your family members would enjoy.
You can add more foods or change some of your ideas after sharing with classmates.

Stop and Discuss

1.   Which meal was easiest to plan? Why?
2.   Check how your daily plans compare to the Healthy Eating Pyramid guidelines. Do your data tables have 6 to 11 servings of bread, cereal, rice, and pasta? 3 to 5 servings of vegetables? 2 to 4 servings of fruits? 2 to 3 servings of milk, yogurt, and cheese? 2 to 3 servings of meat, poultry, fish, dry beans, eggs, and nuts? only a few fats and sweets? If your plans don't stack up, make any necessary changes.
3.   Do you think you and your family could eat this way forever? Why or why not?
4.   Does eating a more nutritious diet mean that you can never eat high-fat, high-sugar foods, such as ice cream, cookies, pie, or cake?

WRAP UP

Plan a "Healthy Eating Party" for your class and another class. Decide which nutritious foods you could serve at the party that the other students will like. Plan ways to tell your guests about why each food is a healthy choice. (You might have a label beside each food identifying the food and what makes that food healthy, such as "This food is low in fat.") Decide who will bring the party foods and/or who will prepare them. During the party, you might ask your guests to rate the party foods in order from the one they like the most to the one they like the least and to give you reasons for their choices.

Make a "Healthy Eating Party" recipe booklet by writing the favorite recipes and foods on paper and stapling the papers into a booklet. Give a copy of the booklet to your guests and take a copy home to help you and your family plan menus and parties for other occasions.

INVOLVING FAMILY MEMBERS

Take home the Healthy Meals Data Tables and share them with your family members. Ask them if they would be willing to try these menus for two days. If so, take the data tables with you on your next shopping trip and buy the foods you need. Read the food labels you buy to check that your choices are healthy ones. If family members disagree with your choices, ask them to help you make changes in the menus that include foods they like but that are still healthy choices.

After you eat those meals, discuss what the family thinks about them. Did they taste good? Did they satisfy their hunger? Did they feel better after eating according to the Guidelines for Healthy Eating? Would they be willing to plan more healthy meals? Continue to encourage your family members to make healthy food choices whenever possible.